Fashion Startup F(

Strategies for Launching a Clothing Brand

Oscar Moses

Fashion Startup Foundations
© Copyright 2023 by Oscar Moses
All rights reserved

without permission or backing by the trademark owner. All trademarks and brands within this book are for clarifying purposes only and are owned by the owners themselves, not affiliated with this document.

TABLE OF CONTENTS

CHAPTER 1: INTRODUCTION TO FASHION ENTREPRENEURSHIP

Fashion entrepreneurship is an exhilarating journey that marries creativity with commerce, style with strategy, and dreams with determination. In this chapter, we'll embark on a voyage into the vibrant world of fashion startups. We'll explore the essential facets of this industry and discover the driving forces behind success: passion and persistence.

The Exciting World of Fashion Startups

Imagine a world where creativity knows no bounds, where the art of design meets the science of business, and where the runway and the boardroom are one and the same. Welcome to the thrilling universe of fashion startups.

Fashion startups are the beating heart of the industry. They are the birthplaces of innovation, the creators of trends, and the disruptors of tradition. Whether you aspire to launch your clothing line, design accessories, or redefine sustainable fashion, a fashion startup is the gateway to realizing your vision.

What sets fashion entrepreneurship apart is its dynamic nature. The fashion world thrives on change, and startups are at the forefront of this evolution. They challenge conventions, experiment with new materials, embrace technology, and explore diverse markets. They breathe life into concepts and give wings to creativity. Fashion startups are where the magic happens.

Here are a few aspects that make the world of fashion startups so exciting:

Innovation: Startups are the engines of innovation in fashion. They introduce fresh ideas, styles, and technologies that push the boundaries of the industry.

Diversity: Fashion startups represent a kaleidoscope of styles, cultures, and perspectives. They celebrate individuality and cater to unique tastes and needs.

Entrepreneurship: The entrepreneurial spirit is at its peak in fashion startups. They embody the relentless pursuit of success, even in a fiercely competitive industry.

Global Reach: Fashion startups have the power to transcend borders. With e-commerce and digital marketing, your fashion brand can reach a global audience.

Sustainability: Many startups are leading the charge in sustainable and ethical fashion, aligning their values with the concerns of our planet and society.

Understanding the Fashion Industry

Before diving headfirst into the fashion startup world, it's crucial to understand the broader context—the fashion industry itself. The fashion industry encompasses a complex network of individuals, organizations, and activities dedicated to the creation, production, distribution, and consumption of fashion products.

Key components of the fashion industry include:

Design: The creative process of conceiving, sketching, and developing fashion products. Designers are the visionaries behind fashion brands.

Manufacturing: The production of clothing and accessories. Manufacturers transform design ideas into tangible products.

Distribution: The supply chain and logistics that deliver fashion products to consumers. This includes everything from local boutiques to global online retailers.

Retail: The point of sale where consumers discover, try on, and purchase fashion products. Retail encompasses physical stores and e-commerce platforms.

Marketing and Promotion: The strategies and tactics used to promote and sell fashion products. Marketing involves advertising, public relations, and branding.

Consumer Behavior: The study of how consumers choose, purchase, and interact with fashion products. Understanding consumer behavior is critical for fashion entrepreneurs.

Trends and Forecasting: The analysis of fashion trends and predictions for future consumer preferences. Trends shape product development and marketing strategies.

Sustainability and Ethics: A growing focus on eco-friendly and socially responsible practices within the fashion industry.

Navigating the fashion industry requires a grasp of its intricate web of components and a sensitivity to its ever-evolving dynamics. Success in fashion entrepreneurship is contingent on your ability to find your place within this ecosystem, create a distinctive brand, and satisfy the ever-changing desires of your target audience.

Passion and Persistence: The Keys to Success

Fashion entrepreneurship is not for the faint of heart. It's a journey laden with challenges, uncertainties, and fierce competition. However, two qualities stand out as the cornerstones of success: passion and persistence.

Passion: Fashion startups thrive on passion. It's the fuel that ignites creativity, drives innovation, and fuels the determination to overcome obstacles. Passion is what keeps you going when the going gets tough. It's the love for fashion and the unwavering belief in your vision that sets your startup on a path to success. Whether you're passionate about sustainable fashion, avant-garde design, or making fashion more inclusive, your passion is your guiding star.

Persistence: The road to fashion entrepreneurship is rife with challenges, setbacks, and failures. It's the entrepreneurs who persist, who adapt, who keep learning and evolving, who ultimately succeed. Persistence involves resilience, tenacity, and the ability to embrace failure as a stepping stone to success. It's the determination to get back up, learn from mistakes, and keep moving forward. The world of fashion startups is a testament to the power of persistence.

Fashion entrepreneurship is a thrilling rollercoaster ride through a world of style and substance. As you embark on this journey, remember that it's your passion for fashion and your unwavering persistence that will be your greatest allies. This book is your guide to not only surviving but thriving in the exciting world of fashion startups. Get ready to explore the world of design, manufacturing, distribution, retail, and all the unique challenges and rewards that come with it.

Chapter 2: Conceptualizing Your Fashion Brand

In the vast and diverse world of fashion, where every garment tells a story and every accessory speaks of personality, conceptualizing your fashion brand is a journey of self-discovery and innovation. This chapter explores the essential steps to bring your brand to life—finding your niche in the market, crafting your brand identity, and mastering the art of storytelling through a compelling brand narrative.

Finding Your Niche in the Market

The fashion industry is like a bustling marketplace, with countless stalls and wares, each catering to a specific group of customers. To establish your fashion brand, you must find your niche—a unique and distinct corner of this marketplace where your products will shine and your brand will resonate with a specific audience.

Here's how to identify your niche:

Research the Market: Begin by researching the fashion market to understand the trends, customer preferences, and gaps that exist. Investigate the competition and identify underserved segments or untapped opportunities.

Identify Your Target Audience: Your target audience is the group of people who will be most interested in and benefit from your fashion products. Consider factors like age, gender, style preferences, and lifestyle when defining your ideal customers.

Niche Down: Don't be afraid to narrow down your niche further. For example, if you want to create women's clothing, you could specialize in sustainable activewear for eco-conscious women who love outdoor activities. The more specific your niche, the easier it is to stand out.

Unique Selling Proposition (USP): Determine what sets your brand apart. Is it your design aesthetic, your use of sustainable materials, or your commitment to fair trade? Your USP is the reason why your target audience should choose your brand over others.

Validation: Once you've identified your niche, validate it. Reach out to potential customers, gather feedback, and see if there is demand for what you plan to offer.

Passion and Knowledge: Choose a niche that aligns with your passions and expertise. Being genuinely enthusiastic about your niche will make your journey more enjoyable and authentic.

Crafting Your Brand Identity

A strong brand identity is the essence of your fashion brand. It's what differentiates you in a crowded market, and it's what customers connect with. Your brand identity encompasses your brand name, logo, color palette, typography, and the overall visual and emotional presentation of your brand. Here's how to craft your brand identity:

Brand Name: Choose a brand name that's memorable, relevant to your niche, and available for trademark. The name should reflect your brand's personality and values.

Logo Design: Design a unique and eye-catching logo that represents your brand. The logo should be versatile, working well on clothing tags, business cards, and your website.

Color Palette: Select a color palette that resonates with your niche and aligns with your brand's identity. Colors evoke emotions and can set the tone for your brand.

Typography: Choose fonts that complement your brand's style. Different fonts convey different feelings. For instance, a sleek, modern font may be suitable for a high-end fashion brand, while a playful font might work for a children's clothing line.

Visual Elements: Consider other visual elements like patterns, textures, and imagery that will be associated with your brand. These elements should be consistent across your branding materials.

Brand Personality: Define the personality of your brand. Is it sophisticated, eco-friendly, edgy, or playful? Your brand's personality should align with the preferences of your target audience.

Brand Voice: Develop a consistent brand voice for your communication. Your brand's tone and language should resonate with your customers. For example, a luxury brand might have a formal and elegant voice, while a streetwear brand could use a more casual and urban tone.

Storytelling: Your brand identity should tell a story. This story can be about your journey, your commitment to sustainability, or the inspiration behind your designs. Stories create a deeper connection with customers.

The Art of Storytelling: Brand Narrative

In the fashion world, every brand has a story to tell. The art of storytelling is a powerful tool for establishing an emotional connection with your customers. Your brand narrative is the story that communicates your brand's values, mission, and the inspiration behind your designs.

Here's how to create a compelling brand narrative:

Brand Origin: Share the story of how your brand came into existence. What inspired you to start your fashion label? What challenges have you overcome? These stories make your brand relatable and human.

Mission and Values: Clearly state your brand's mission and values. If sustainability is a core value, communicate how your brand incorporates eco-friendly practices in its processes.

Design Inspiration: Describe the inspiration behind your designs. Whether it's nature, a specific culture, or personal experiences, sharing your creative journey helps customers connect with your products on a deeper level.

Customer Stories: Share stories and testimonials from satisfied customers. This social proof adds credibility to your brand.

Content Marketing: Use various content marketing channels like blogs, social media, and videos to tell your brand's story. Consistent storytelling helps keep your brand in the minds of your customers.

Brand Visuals: Ensure that your brand visuals, such as your logo and marketing materials, align with your brand narrative. These visuals should echo the story you're telling.

Your brand narrative is an ongoing conversation with your audience. It shapes your brand's personality, builds trust, and engages customers on a personal level. Effective storytelling can transform first-time buyers into loyal, lifelong customers.

In this chapter, we've explored the foundational steps of conceptualizing your fashion brand. It's a process of finding your niche, crafting a strong brand identity, and mastering the art of storytelling. These elements form the core of your brand's identity and are crucial in establishing your presence in the fashion industry.

Chapter 3: Market Research and Analysis

In the world of fashion entrepreneurship, understanding your market is paramount. Chapter 3 delves into the critical aspects of market research and analysis, including the identification of your target audience, the analysis of market trends, and the assessment of your competitive landscape. These elements are the compass guiding your fashion startup toward success.

Identifying Your Target Audience

Your fashion brand's success hinges on your ability to connect with the right customers—those who resonate with your designs, values, and mission. Identifying your target audience is the first step on your path to building a loyal customer base.

Here's how to pinpoint your ideal customers:

Demographics: Begin by defining the demographic characteristics of your target audience. Consider age, gender, location, income, and other relevant factors. For instance, are you designing for young urban professionals, busy parents, or seniors who appreciate classic styles?

Psychographics: Dive deeper into your audience's psychology. What are their lifestyles, interests, values, and aspirations? Understanding the psychographics of your customers helps tailor your brand's messaging and offerings to their desires.

Behavioral Insights: Analyze consumer behavior. What are their shopping habits? How do they discover new fashion brands? This information guides your marketing and sales strategies.

Problem Solving: Identify the problems or needs your fashion brand can address for your target audience. This might involve creating eco-friendly clothing for environmentally conscious consumers or stylish, functional attire for outdoor enthusiasts.

Customer Personas: Create customer personas, detailed profiles of your ideal customers. Give them names and backstories. Personas help you visualize and empathize with your audience.

Survey and Feedback: Conduct surveys, interviews, or focus groups with potential customers to gather their feedback and insights. These direct interactions provide invaluable information.

Competition Analysis: Study your competitors to identify gaps or underserved segments in the market. These gaps might present opportunities for your brand to shine.

Testing and Validation: Once you've identified your target audience, test your assumptions. Launch a small collection or conduct a pilot campaign to validate your understanding of your customers.

By identifying your target audience with precision, you can tailor your fashion brand's products, marketing, and messaging to speak directly to the people most likely to embrace your designs.

Analyzing Market Trends

The fashion industry is ever-evolving, with trends that shift and change with the seasons. Keeping a finger on the pulse of these trends is vital for your fashion startup's relevance and success.

Here's how to analyze market trends effectively:

Fashion Forecasting: Invest time in fashion forecasting, which involves studying fashion shows, fashion magazines, and influential designers' collections. Identify emerging trends in colors, styles, and materials.

Consumer Insights: Pay attention to consumer behavior and preferences. Analyze data from fashion retailers, e-commerce platforms, and social media to uncover what consumers are currently drawn to.

Sustainability: Keep a close eye on sustainability trends. Consumers increasingly prioritize eco-friendly and ethical fashion. Understanding sustainable practices can set your brand apart.

Global Trends: Don't limit your trend analysis to your immediate surroundings. Global trends influence the fashion world. Fashion capitals like New York, Paris, Milan, and London often set the stage for global fashion.

Technology: Embrace technology trends. E-commerce, augmented reality (AR), and virtual reality (VR) are reshaping the fashion industry. Understanding how technology impacts your niche is crucial.

Seasonal Awareness: Recognize the seasonality of fashion. Different seasons demand different styles and materials. Stay ahead of the curve by preparing collections well in advance.

Competitor Trends: Analyze your competitors' collections and marketing strategies. What are they emphasizing, and how can your brand differentiate itself?

Data Analytics: Utilize data analytics to track customer behavior and preferences. Data-driven insights can reveal emerging trends and help tailor your offerings.

Trend analysis is not about blindly following what's popular but about understanding the evolving landscape of fashion and how your brand can authentically adapt to it. By staying attuned to market trends, you can create collections that are not only trendy but also aligned with your audience's desires.

Competitive Landscape Assessment

Understanding your competitors is essential to positioning your fashion brand effectively. Competitive landscape assessment involves evaluating the strengths, weaknesses, strategies, and market presence of your competition.

Here's how to conduct a competitive landscape assessment:

Identify Key Competitors: List your direct and indirect competitors. Direct competitors share a similar target audience and product offering, while indirect competitors might serve the same audience with different products.

SWOT Analysis: Perform a SWOT (Strengths, Weaknesses, Opportunities, Threats) analysis for each competitor. Assess their brand positioning, product quality, pricing strategies, and marketing efforts.

Unique Selling Proposition (USP): Identify what sets your competitors apart. Do they emphasize sustainability, affordability, luxury, or innovation? Understanding their USPs helps you find your own differentiators.

Market Share: Determine the market share of your competitors. Are there gaps or underserved segments that your brand can address?

Pricing Strategy: Analyze your competitors' pricing strategies. Are they positioned as luxury brands, mid-market, or budget-friendly? Your pricing should align with your brand's positioning.

Marketing and Promotion: Study your competitors' marketing efforts. How do they engage with their audience? What social media channels do they use? What content resonates with their customers?

Customer Reviews and Feedback: Investigate customer reviews and feedback for your competitors. This information can reveal common customer pain points and preferences.

Distribution Channels: Understand where and how your competitors sell their products. Are they primarily e-commerce-based, or do they have physical stores?

A thorough competitive landscape assessment helps you position your brand strategically. It allows you to uncover opportunities, address gaps in the market, and emphasize your unique strengths and value proposition.

In this chapter, we've explored the essential steps of market research and analysis in the context of fashion entrepreneurship. Identifying your target audience, analyzing market trends, and assessing the competitive landscape are pivotal elements in establishing a successful fashion startup. With this knowledge, you'll be well-prepared to create fashion products that resonate with your customers and position your brand effectively in the marketplace.

CHAPTER 4: CREATING A WINNING BUSINESS PLAN

In the realm of fashion entrepreneurship, a well-crafted business plan serves as your roadmap to success. This chapter delves into the critical aspects of developing a solid business plan, including the creation of financial projections and budgeting, as well as exploring various funding options to bring your fashion startup to life.

Developing a Solid Business Plan

A business plan is the foundational document that outlines your fashion brand's strategy, goals, and how you plan to achieve them. It serves as a detailed blueprint for your business, providing clarity to you, your team, and potential investors.

Here's how to develop a solid business plan for your fashion startup:

Executive Summary: Begin with an executive summary that offers a concise overview of your business, including your mission, vision, and a summary of what your brand represents.

Company Description: Detail the nature of your fashion business. Explain your brand's story, values, and what sets it apart from the competition.

Market Analysis: Present a comprehensive analysis of your target market, including size, demographics, and consumer behavior. Highlight market trends and your target audience's preferences.

Competitive Analysis: Analyze your competitors, their strengths, weaknesses, and market positioning. Discuss how your brand will differentiate itself.

Organization and Management: Describe your organizational structure and management team. Outline the roles and responsibilities of key team members.

Product Line: Detail your fashion product offerings, including your design philosophy and how your products address market needs.

Sales and Marketing Strategy: Explain your sales and marketing strategies, including how you plan to reach and engage your target audience.

Funding Request: If you're seeking investment, clearly state your funding requirements, how you'll use the funds, and what investors can expect in return.

Financial Projections: Provide detailed financial projections, including income statements, balance sheets, and cash flow statements.

Appendices: Include any additional information or documentation that supports your business plan.

Remember that your business plan is a living document. It will evolve as your fashion startup grows and adapts to the changing market. Regularly revisit and update your plan to ensure it remains aligned with your goals and circumstances.

Financial Projections and Budgeting

Financial projections and budgeting are core components of your business plan. They provide a snapshot of your fashion startup's financial health and potential future performance.

Here's how to approach financial projections and budgeting effectively:

Sales Projections: Estimate your expected sales based on your market research and target audience. Consider factors like seasonality and trends.

Expenses: Create a detailed list of your anticipated expenses. This should include manufacturing costs, marketing expenses, overhead, salaries, and any other costs related to running your business.

Income Statements: Develop income statements (also known as profit and loss statements) that outline your revenue, costs, and profit margins. These statements help you understand your profitability.

Balance Sheets: Balance sheets provide an overview of your company's financial position, including assets, liabilities, and equity. This is essential for investors and lenders.

Cash Flow Projections: Cash flow projections illustrate how money flows in and out of your business. It's vital for managing working capital and ensuring you can meet financial obligations.

Break-Even Analysis: Determine the point at which your total revenue equals your total expenses, resulting in neither profit nor loss. This is a crucial milestone for your startup.

Budgeting: Create a detailed budget that outlines your monthly and annual expenses. Budgeting helps you manage your finances effectively and avoid overspending.

Financial Assumptions: Clearly state the assumptions behind your financial projections. This transparency helps investors and lenders understand the basis for your numbers.

Financial projections and budgeting are not merely exercises in number-crunching; they are the instruments that guide your financial decisions. They help you set achievable targets, identify potential financial challenges, and ensure that your fashion startup remains financially sound.

Funding Your Fashion Startup

Securing funding for your fashion startup is a pivotal step in bringing your vision to life. Fashion entrepreneurship often requires initial investments to cover product development, manufacturing, marketing, and other expenses. Here are some options for funding your fashion startup:

Bootstrapping: Bootstrapping involves using your personal savings or revenue generated by your business to fund its growth. It provides full control over your business but may limit your initial scale.

Crowdfunding: Platforms like Kickstarter and Indiegogo allow you to present your fashion startup to the public and raise funds from individual backers.

Angel Investors: Angel investors are individuals who provide capital in exchange for equity in your business. They often bring expertise and connections in addition to funding.

Venture Capital: Venture capital firms invest in startups with high growth potential. They typically seek larger equity stakes in exchange for substantial funding.

Small Business Loans: Many government agencies and banks offer small business loans to entrepreneurs. These loans can provide significant capital for your startup.

Grants: Explore grants available from government agencies and foundations that support specific industries or causes, such as sustainability or innovation.

Accelerators and Incubators: These programs offer funding, mentorship, and resources to startups in exchange for equity. They can provide guidance and connections in addition to capital.

Partnerships and Collaborations: Consider forming partnerships or collaborations with established fashion brands. These partnerships can bring financial support and exposure to your startup.

Family and Friends: Some entrepreneurs secure funding from family and friends who believe in their vision. However, this approach should be approached with care to maintain personal relationships.

Personal Savings: Utilizing your own savings or assets is a common way to fund your startup, giving you full control and eliminating the need to give up equity.

When choosing a funding option, consider the stage of your fashion startup, your financial needs, and your long-term goals. It's essential to weigh the benefits and trade-offs of each option and tailor your funding strategy to align with your unique circumstances.

In this chapter, we've explored the critical elements of creating a winning business plan for your fashion startup. Developing a solid business plan, crafting financial projections and budgets, and exploring various funding options are essential steps in setting your fashion brand on the path to success. Your business plan is the guiding document that ensures your business stays focused on its objectives and financial health. With a well-defined plan, you'll be better prepared to navigate the complex landscape of fashion entrepreneurship and make your vision a reality.

CHAPTER 5: LEGAL AND REGULATORY CONSIDERATIONS

In the realm of fashion entrepreneurship, navigating the legal and regulatory landscape is crucial for protecting your brand, ensuring your business operates within the confines of the law, and complying with industry standards. This chapter explores the key legal and regulatory aspects, including trademarks and intellectual property, business structure and registration, and compliance with industry standards.

Trademarks and Intellectual Property

Intellectual property (IP) protection is paramount in the fashion industry, where creativity and innovation drive success. Trademarks, copyrights, and patents safeguard your brand's unique assets and creations. Here's a breakdown of these crucial aspects:

Trademarks: Trademarks protect your brand's name, logo, and any distinctive symbols or elements associated with your business. Registering a trademark provides legal ownership and exclusive rights to use these assets, preventing others from using similar marks.

Registration: Consult with a trademark attorney or use the United States Patent and Trademark Office (USPTO) to register your trademarks. Registration ensures legal protection.

Enforcement: Regularly monitor the marketplace to identify any unauthorized use of your trademarks. Take legal action against infringers to protect your brand's integrity.

Copyrights: Copyrights protect original creative works, including fashion designs, patterns, and marketing materials. While fashion itself is not directly copyrightable, unique textile patterns, illustrations, and promotional materials can be.

Registration: Copyright registration is not required but provides additional legal protection. Register your copyrights with the U.S. Copyright Office to establish a clear record of ownership.

Licensing: If you wish to collaborate with other brands or individuals, consider licensing your copyrighted materials. Licensing agreements should outline terms and compensation.

Design Patents: Design patents protect the unique, non-functional, ornamental design of an item. While less common in fashion, they can be used to protect distinctive accessories or elements of clothing.

Intellectual Property Agreements: When working with designers, artists, or collaborators, have clear intellectual property agreements in place. These documents define ownership, licensing, and usage rights.

Protecting your intellectual property is a long-term investment in your brand's integrity and value. It ensures that your unique designs and assets remain your exclusive property and that others cannot profit from your creativity without permission.

Business Structure and Registration

Choosing the right business structure and completing the necessary registrations is essential for establishing your fashion brand as a legal entity. The structure you select can affect taxation, liability, and business operations. Here are some considerations:

Sole Proprietorship: In a sole proprietorship, you are the sole owner of your business. It's the simplest structure, but you have personal liability for business debts.

Partnership: A partnership involves two or more individuals sharing ownership and responsibility. There are general and limited partnerships, each with different liability implications.

Limited Liability Company (LLC): An LLC offers personal liability protection, separating your personal assets from your business assets. It provides flexibility in management and taxation.

Corporation: A corporation is a separate legal entity from its owners. It offers strong liability protection but involves complex record-keeping and formalities.

Business Registration: Register your fashion startup with the appropriate state and local authorities. This process typically involves choosing a business name and filing the necessary documents.

Employer Identification Number (EIN): Obtain an EIN from the Internal Revenue Service (IRS) for tax purposes, even if you don't have employees. This number is necessary for tax reporting.

Business Licenses and Permits: Determine the specific licenses and permits required for your fashion startup based on your location and the nature of your business.

Operating Agreements and Bylaws: Create operating agreements (for LLCs) or bylaws (for corporations) that outline how your business will operate, including decision-making processes and ownership structure.

Selecting the right business structure and completing registrations and filings can be complex, and it's advisable to consult with legal professionals or business advisors to ensure that you make the best choices for your fashion startup.

Compliance with Industry Standards

The fashion industry is subject to various industry standards and regulations that ensure the safety, quality, and ethical practices of fashion businesses.

Here are some key areas of compliance:

Sustainability: The fashion industry is increasingly focused on sustainability and ethical practices. Ensure that your production methods, materials, and sourcing align with sustainable standards and certifications.

Textile Regulations: Textiles used in clothing must meet safety and quality standards. Be aware of regulations regarding materials, dyes, and labeling.

Safety Standards: Children's clothing and accessories have specific safety standards. Compliance with these standards is crucial if your fashion startup produces items for children.

Ethical Manufacturing: Uphold ethical manufacturing practices, including fair wages, safe working conditions, and no child labor. Certification from organizations like Fair Trade USA can help demonstrate your commitment.

Consumer Protection Laws: Comply with consumer protection laws, such as return policies, warranties, and accurate product descriptions. This ensures customer trust and satisfaction.

Labeling and Packaging: Labeling requirements, including care instructions and country of origin, must be met for all clothing and accessories.

Trade Regulations: Understand international trade regulations if your fashion startup operates in the global market. Tariffs, customs requirements, and trade agreements can impact your business.

Intellectual Property: Respect the intellectual property rights of others, including trademarks and copyrights. Avoid using copyrighted materials without permission.

Ensuring compliance with industry standards and regulations is not just a matter of legality but also a way to build trust and credibility with consumers. It demonstrates your commitment to ethical and responsible business practices, which can be a strong selling point for your fashion brand.

In this chapter, we've explored the essential legal and regulatory considerations for fashion entrepreneurship. Protecting your intellectual property, selecting the right business structure, and ensuring compliance with industry standards are pivotal for the long-term success of your fashion startup. These aspects lay the legal foundation for your business, protect your brand's assets, and contribute to your brand's reputation for quality and integrity.

CHAPTER 6: SOURCING MATERIALS AND PRODUCTION

In the world of fashion entrepreneurship, sourcing materials and overseeing production are vital steps in bringing your creative vision to life. This chapter delves into the key aspects of sourcing fabrics and materials, choosing the right manufacturers, and ensuring quality control and production oversight for your fashion startup.

Sourcing Fabrics and Materials

The selection of fabrics and materials is at the heart of fashion design. The materials you choose affect the quality, aesthetics, and sustainability of your products. Here's how to source fabrics and materials effectively:

Material Research: Begin by researching different materials, including their properties, sustainability, and suitability for your designs. Consider factors like texture, weight, and durability.

Sourcing Options: Identify reliable suppliers and fabric mills. This may include local textile manufacturers, global suppliers, or sustainable and eco-friendly material sources.

Quality Assessment: Request fabric samples to assess their quality. Test fabrics for colorfastness, shrinkage, and wear resistance. Verify whether they meet industry standards and regulations.

Minimum Order Quantities (MOQs): Understand the MOQs set by material suppliers. These are the minimum quantities you must order, and they can impact your production costs.

Cost Considerations: Evaluate the cost of materials in relation to your budget and pricing strategy. High-quality and sustainable materials may come at a premium.

Sustainability: Consider eco-friendly and sustainable materials, such as organic cotton, recycled fabrics, or cruelty-free alternatives. Aligning with sustainable practices can enhance your brand's appeal.

Supplier Relationships: Build strong relationships with material suppliers. Effective communication and reliability are essential for long-term partnerships.

Material Swatches: Create material swatch books to showcase your fabric choices to clients and manufacturers. These swatches serve as a reference for design and production.

Choosing the right materials is a creative and strategic process that involves balancing your design vision, sustainability goals, budget, and quality standards.

Choosing the Right Manufacturers

Selecting the right manufacturers is a critical decision that directly impacts the quality and consistency of your fashion products. Here's how to make informed choices:

Manufacturer Research: Research potential manufacturers and production facilities. Consider factors like location, production capacity, and specialization.

Quality Assessment: Evaluate the quality of their work by reviewing their portfolio, samples, and finished products. Look for manufacturers experienced in your niche.

Compliance and Certification: Ensure that manufacturers adhere to industry standards, ethical practices, and quality certifications. This may include certifications for sustainable and fair trade production.

Communication and Transparency: Open and transparent communication with manufacturers is key. Discuss your requirements, quality standards, and production timelines.

Negotiation and Contracts: Negotiate terms and contracts carefully. Address pricing, production timelines, quality control, and order volumes in your agreements.

Factory Visits: Whenever possible, visit the manufacturing facility to assess working conditions, quality control, and production processes firsthand.

Sample Production: Before mass production, request sample products to validate quality, design, and fit.

Make any necessary adjustments based on these samples.

Ongoing Relationship: Maintain a collaborative relationship with your manufacturers. Clear communication and trust are essential for smooth production.

The right manufacturers can become valued partners in your fashion business, helping you bring your designs to life efficiently and with the quality your customers expect.

Quality Control and Production Oversight

Quality control and production oversight are essential to ensure that your fashion products meet the standards you've set. It's an ongoing process that begins at the material sourcing stage and continues throughout production. Here's how to implement effective quality control:

Quality Standards: Establish clear quality standards and criteria for your products. Communicate these standards to your manufacturers.

Inspections: Conduct regular inspections at different stages of production, from material arrival to finished goods. Inspect for defects, consistency, and adherence to design.

Documentation: Keep detailed records of quality control assessments, including photographs and written reports. This documentation is essential for tracking improvements and addressing issues.

Feedback Loop: Maintain open communication with manufacturers. Provide constructive feedback and work together to resolve any quality-related issues.

Testing and Certification: If your products require testing or certification, ensure these processes are integrated into your production schedule.

Prototyping: Consider creating prototypes or samples of new designs to identify potential issues before they go into mass production.

Customer Feedback: Consider gathering feedback from customers on product quality and fit. Use this information to make improvements.

Quality control is an ongoing process that should be embedded in your production workflow. Consistent oversight helps maintain the integrity of your brand and ensures that customers receive products that meet their expectations.

CHAPTER 7: DESIGN AND PRODUCT DEVELOPMENT

The heart of the fashion industry lies in the process of design and product development. This chapter dives into the critical aspects of bringing your creative vision to life, from sketching your designs to sample development and prototyping, and ultimately refining your fashion collection for your startup.

Sketching Your Designs

The design process is where your creative ideas take shape. Sketching is the first step in translating your vision into tangible designs. Here's how to approach sketching your fashion creations:

Conceptualize Your Vision: Begin with a clear vision of what you want to create. Consider the theme, inspiration, and overall aesthetic of your collection.

Sketching Tools: Invest in quality sketching tools, including pencils, markers, sketchbooks, and digital design software, if you prefer to work digitally.

Silhouettes and Details: Start with rough sketches to define silhouettes, proportions, and key design elements. Focus on outlines and the overall shape.

Fabric and Color: Consider the fabrics and color palettes that will bring your designs to life. Use color swatches and fabric samples to plan your designs accurately.

Iterate and Refine: Don't be afraid to iterate and refine your sketches. Experiment with variations of your designs to find the best possible outcome.

Technical Drawings: Create technical drawings that provide detailed measurements and construction information. These drawings are essential for pattern making and production.

Storytelling: Your sketches should tell a story about your collection. They should convey the mood, inspiration, and style you aim to capture.

Feedback: Share your sketches with peers, mentors, or fashion professionals to gather feedback and insights.

Sketching is not just a preliminary step; it's the foundation of your fashion collection. It's where your ideas transform into visual representations that guide the rest of the product development process.

Sample Development and Prototyping

Once your sketches are ready, it's time to turn them into physical samples. Sample development and prototyping allow you to test your designs, materials, and construction methods. Here's how to approach this stage:

Pattern Making: Create patterns for your designs. Patterns are templates used to cut and sew fabrics. They must be accurate and reflect the design details.

Material Selection: Choose the materials that match your sketches. Work closely with fabric suppliers to ensure you get the right fabrics for your designs.

Sample Production: Collaborate with manufacturers to produce sample garments. These samples should be true representations of your designs and must meet your quality standards.

Fittings and Adjustments: Conduct fittings to evaluate the fit and comfort of your designs. Make any necessary adjustments to improve the fit.

Quality Assessment: Assess the quality of the samples rigorously. Check for stitching, seams, finishing, and overall construction.

Feedback Loop: Maintain open communication with the manufacturers and your team. Address any issues or concerns that arise during the sample development process.

Photography and Documentation: Take clear photographs and document the details of your samples. This documentation serves as a reference for production.

Sample development and prototyping are stages where you can identify and rectify any design or production issues before committing to mass production. It's a critical phase for ensuring that your final collection aligns with your original vision.

Refining Your Collection

The design process is rarely linear. It involves continuous refinement and adjustments. Once you have your samples, you can further refine your collection:

Feedback Integration: Use feedback from fittings, quality assessments, and team discussions to refine your designs.

Material Tweaks: If necessary, make adjustments to the materials and fabrics based on the performance of your samples.

Cost Analysis: Analyze the cost implications of your designs, materials, and production methods. Ensure that your collection remains within budget.

Design Consistency: Ensure that your designs align with the overall aesthetic and theme of your collection. Consistency is key in creating a cohesive collection.

Finalizing Technical Drawings: Make any final adjustments to your technical drawings to reflect the precise design details.

Production Planning: Plan for mass production, considering order quantities, production timelines, and quality control measures.

Refinement is an ongoing process, and it's essential for creating a collection that not only captures your creative vision but also meets practical and market requirements.

In this chapter, we've explored the pivotal stages of design and product development for your fashion startup. From sketching your designs to sample development and prototyping, and ultimately refining your collection, each step contributes to bringing your creative vision to life. These processes require creativity, attention to detail, and an iterative approach to ensure that your final collection is not only aesthetically pleasing but also functional and well-crafted.

CHAPTER 8: BRANDING AND MARKETING STRATEGIES

In the highly competitive world of fashion entrepreneurship, building a strong brand and crafting effective marketing strategies are vital for establishing your presence in the market. This chapter explores the key aspects of creating your brand's visual identity, developing a comprehensive marketing plan, and executing both online and offline marketing efforts to drive success for your fashion startup.

Building Your Brand's Visual Identity

Your brand's visual identity is the face of your fashion startup. It's the first impression you make on your target audience, and it plays a crucial role in shaping your brand's identity. Here's how to build a compelling visual identity for your fashion brand:

Logo Design: Create a unique and memorable logo that encapsulates the essence of your brand. Consider working with a professional graphic designer to ensure a high-quality design.

Color Palette: Choose a color palette that resonates with your brand's personality and the emotions you want to evoke in your customers. Consistency in color use is key.

Typography: Select fonts that align with your brand's style and message. Consider how typography enhances the readability and aesthetics of your materials.

Visual Elements: Define any additional visual elements such as patterns, motifs, or icons that are unique to your brand and can be used across your marketing materials.

Photography and Imagery: Invest in high-quality photography that showcases your products and tells your brand's story. Consistency in style and image quality is essential.

Branding Guidelines: Create branding guidelines that detail how your visual identity elements should be used in different contexts. This helps maintain consistency.

Packaging Design: Pay attention to the design of your product packaging. It should reflect your brand's identity and contribute to the overall brand experience.

In-Store or Online Presentation: Ensure that your physical retail space or e-commerce website is designed to reflect your brand's visual identity. This consistency reinforces your brand image.

Storytelling: Your visual identity should convey a narrative about your brand. Use it to communicate your brand's values, mission, and unique selling points.

Adaptation and Evolution: Be open to making adjustments to your visual identity as your brand grows and evolves. Your visual identity should be able to adapt to changing market trends and customer preferences.

A well-crafted visual identity not only attracts customers but also fosters brand recognition and loyalty. It's the visual representation of your brand's personality and what it stands for.

Crafting a Marketing Plan

Creating a marketing plan is a critical step in reaching your target audience and promoting your fashion startup. A comprehensive marketing plan should encompass a mix of strategies to maximize your brand's exposure. Here's how to craft an effective marketing plan:

Market Research: Begin with in-depth market research to understand your target audience, competition, and industry trends. This research forms the foundation of your marketing strategy.

Set Clear Objectives: Define clear and achievable marketing objectives. What do you want to accomplish with your marketing efforts, and how will you measure success?

Target Audience: Identify and create detailed buyer personas to guide your marketing strategies. Tailor your messaging and channels to your specific audience segments.

Channel Selection: Choose the marketing channels that are most effective for reaching your target audience. This may include social media, email marketing, content marketing, SEO, paid advertising, and influencer partnerships.

Content Strategy: Develop a content strategy that provides value to your audience. Create high-quality content, including blog posts, videos, and social media updates that resonate with your target audience.

Budget Allocation: Allocate your marketing budget wisely. Consider the cost of various marketing channels and how they align with your objectives.

Timeline and Scheduling: Create a marketing calendar that outlines the timing of your campaigns, product launches, and promotional efforts. Consistency is key in marketing.

Testing and Optimization: Regularly monitor and analyze the performance of your marketing efforts.

Use data and feedback to make improvements and optimize your strategies.

Collaborations and Partnerships: Explore collaborations with influencers, complementary brands, and fashion bloggers to expand your reach and credibility.

Measure and Adjust: Use analytics and key performance indicators (KPIs) to measure the success of your marketing campaigns. Adjust your strategies based on the data.

Effective marketing is not a one-size-fits-all approach; it requires customization to suit your brand, products, and target audience. Your marketing plan should be adaptable and responsive to market changes and emerging opportunities.

Effective Online and Offline Marketing

Marketing your fashion brand effectively involves a mix of online and offline strategies, each offering unique opportunities to engage with your audience. Here's how to implement both:

Online Marketing:

Social Media: Utilize popular social media platforms like Instagram, Facebook, Pinterest, and TikTok to showcase your products and engage with your audience.

Email Marketing: Build and nurture an email list to communicate directly with your customers. Use email campaigns to share product updates, promotions, and brand stories.

Content Marketing: Create a blog or video content that educates, entertains, or inspires your audience.

This can establish your brand as an authority in the fashion niche.

SEO: Optimize your website and content for search engines to increase organic visibility. A strong SEO strategy can drive free, high-quality traffic to your site.

Paid Advertising: Consider paid advertising on platforms like Google Ads and Facebook Ads to reach a broader audience and target specific demographics.

Offline Marketing:

Pop-Up Shops: Organize temporary pop-up shops or attend local markets and events to connect with your community and showcase your products in person.

Fashion Shows: Host or participate in fashion shows to unveil your latest collections and connect with industry professionals.

Print Media: Advertise in fashion magazines or local newspapers to reach a broader, offline audience.

Influencer and Celebrity Collaborations: Collaborate with local influencers or celebrities to gain exposure through their offline events and activities.

Networking and Partnerships: Attend fashion and business networking events to build relationships with industry professionals, potential partners, and customers.

Fashion Sponsorships: Sponsor fashion-related events or charity fashion shows to align your brand with a particular cause or aesthetic.

In today's digital age, online marketing is essential for reaching a global audience, while offline marketing allows you to connect with local customers and build a physical presence for your brand. A balanced approach leveraging both online and offline strategies can enhance your brand's visibility and impact.

Chapter 9: Establishing an Online Presence

In the digital age, establishing a robust online presence is paramount for the success of your fashion startup. This chapter explores the essential steps for creating a fashionable website, leveraging the power of social media, and embracing e-commerce and online sales platforms to reach a global audience and drive growth.

Creating a Fashionable Website

Your website is the digital storefront of your fashion brand. It's where potential customers learn about your brand, explore your collections, and make purchases. Here's how to create a fashionable website that captures your brand's essence:

Domain and Hosting: Choose a memorable domain name that reflects your brand. Select reliable hosting services to ensure your website's performance and security.

Website Design: Invest in a well-designed website that aligns with your brand's visual identity. Use professional designers and web developers to create a visually appealing and user-friendly site.

Navigation and User Experience: Prioritize user experience. Ensure that your website is easy to navigate, with clear categories and menus that make finding products effortless.

Mobile Optimization: Optimize your website for mobile devices. With a significant portion of online traffic coming from mobile users, it's crucial to provide a seamless mobile experience.

High-Quality Imagery: Use high-resolution, professionally shot images to showcase your products. Include multiple images, zoom features, and product videos for a detailed view.

Product Descriptions: Craft engaging and informative product descriptions. Include details about materials, sizing, care instructions, and any unique features.

Customer Reviews: Encourage customers to leave reviews and ratings for your products. Genuine reviews build trust and credibility.

Secure Payment Options: Provide secure payment options and reassure customers about the safety of their transactions.

Fast Loading Speed: Ensure that your website loads quickly to prevent user frustration and high bounce rates.

Newsletter Sign-Up: Include a newsletter sign-up form to capture email addresses for future marketing efforts.

Contact Information: Make your contact information easily accessible. Include an email address, phone number, and physical address, if applicable.

Blog and Content: Consider starting a blog that complements your products and provides value to your audience. Regularly update your content to keep your website fresh and engaging.

Search Functionality: Implement a robust search feature to help customers find specific products quickly.

Social Media Integration: Link to your social media profiles for easy sharing and cross-promotion.

Analytics: Set up web analytics tools to monitor website traffic, visitor behavior, and sales conversions.

Creating a fashionable website is an investment in your brand's online presence. It's the central hub where customers and potential partners engage with your brand, discover your story, and explore your collections.

Leveraging Social Media

Social media platforms offer a powerful means of connecting with your audience, building a community, and showcasing your fashion brand. Here's how to leverage social media effectively:

Platform Selection: Choose the social media platforms that align with your brand and target audience. Instagram, Facebook, Pinterest, TikTok, and Twitter are popular choices for fashion brands.

Content Planning: Develop a content plan that includes a mix of product showcases, behind-the-scenes glimpses, customer testimonials, and lifestyle shots that resonate with your audience.

Visual Consistency: Maintain a consistent visual identity on your social media profiles. This includes using the same colors, fonts, and imagery as on your website.

Engagement: Engage with your audience by responding to comments, messages, and mentions. Build a rapport with your followers and turn them into loyal customers.

Hashtags: Use relevant and trending hashtags to increase the discoverability of your posts. Create branded hashtags to encourage user-generated content.

Influencer Partnerships: Collaborate with fashion influencers and bloggers who align with your brand. They can introduce your products to their engaged audiences.

User-Generated Content: Encourage customers to share photos and reviews of your products. Repost this user-generated content on your social media profiles.

Paid Advertising: Explore paid advertising options on social media platforms to reach a broader audience and target specific demographics.

Stories and Live Videos: Utilize stories and live video features for real-time engagement and to share exclusive content.

Scheduling Tools: Use social media scheduling tools to plan and automate your posts, ensuring consistent and timely content.

Data Analytics: Analyze the performance of your social media campaigns to understand what works and make adjustments accordingly.

Social media provides a dynamic space to communicate your brand's personality, build relationships with your audience, and stay top-of-mind in a crowded market.

E-commerce and Online Sales Platforms

Online sales platforms are essential for enabling e-commerce and reaching a broader audience. Here are the key steps to establish your fashion brand on e-commerce platforms:

Choose E-commerce Platforms: Select e-commerce platforms that best suit your business. Popular options include Shopify, WooCommerce (for WordPress sites), BigCommerce, and Magento.

Set Up Online Store: Create an online store with features that support your products. This includes setting up product categories, pricing, and payment gateways.

Product Listings: Accurately list your products, including high-quality images, detailed descriptions, and pricing information.

Inventory Management: Implement inventory management tools to keep track of product availability and stock levels.

Shipping and Fulfillment: Determine your shipping and fulfillment processes, including shipping rates, delivery times, and return policies.

Secure Checkout: Ensure that your checkout process is secure and user-friendly to instill confidence in your customers.

Customer Support: Provide clear and accessible customer support through chat, email, or phone to assist customers with inquiries and issues.

Security: Implement security measures, including SSL certificates, to protect customer data and transactions.

Cross-Selling and Upselling: Utilize features that enable cross-selling and upselling to boost your sales revenue.

Mobile Optimization: Ensure that your online store is mobile-optimized for seamless shopping on smartphones and tablets.

Promotions and Discounts: Offer promotions and discounts to incentivize purchases and reward loyal customers.

Data Analysis: Use analytics tools to track user behavior, monitor conversions, and identify opportunities for improvement.

E-commerce platforms facilitate online sales, allowing customers to browse your products, make secure payments, and have items delivered to their doorstep. They provide the convenience that modern consumers seek.

CHAPTER 10: BUILDING DISTRIBUTION CHANNELS

Expanding your fashion startup's distribution channels is essential for reaching a broader audience and increasing your brand's visibility. This chapter explores strategies for both retail and wholesale distribution, the use of pop-up shops and fashion shows, and the benefits of collaborations and partnerships to grow your brand.

Retail and Wholesale Strategies

Retail and wholesale are two primary distribution strategies in the fashion industry, each with its advantages and considerations.

Retail Distribution:

Brick-and-Mortar Stores: Consider opening your own physical retail store. A well-located store can serve as a brand showcase and offer a direct shopping experience to customers.

Consignment Shops: Collaborate with consignment stores to place your products in their inventory. You'll receive payment when the items are sold.

Franchising: If your brand grows significantly, explore franchising opportunities. This allows others to operate stores under your brand's name and guidelines.

Pop-Up Shops: Set up temporary pop-up shops in high-traffic areas, creating buzz and excitement around your brand. These shops are particularly popular during special events or seasons.

Wholesale Distribution:

Retailer Partnerships: Partner with existing retailers to stock your products. This can involve local boutiques, department stores, or online fashion retailers.

Showrooms: Use showrooms to showcase your collections to buyers and secure orders from various retailers.

Distributors: Work with fashion distributors who specialize in connecting brands with retailers. They can help you reach a broader market.

Trade Shows: Participate in fashion trade shows to introduce your brand to potential wholesale buyers and establish business relationships.

Both retail and wholesale distribution can coexist in your brand's distribution strategy, providing you with a diverse set of sales channels.

Pop-Up Shops and Fashion Shows

Pop-up shops and fashion shows are valuable tools to generate excitement and visibility for your brand.

Pop-Up Shops:

Location Selection: Choose strategic locations for your pop-up shops. Consider high-traffic areas, shopping districts, and events.

Visual Merchandising: Create eye-catching visual displays to draw customers in and showcase your products effectively.

Limited-Time Offers: Offer exclusive or limited-time promotions and discounts to incentivize sales.

Engagement Activities: Organize events, workshops, or fashion presentations to engage with your audience and create memorable experiences.

Social Media Promotion: Promote your pop-up shop extensively on social media to attract foot traffic and build anticipation.

Fashion Shows:

Event Planning: Plan fashion shows to debut your latest collections. Consider factors like venue, theme, and timing.

Professional Models: Use professional models to showcase your designs effectively.

Media Coverage: Invite fashion journalists, bloggers, and influencers to cover the event and reach a broader audience.

Ticket Sales: Sell tickets to your fashion show to not only cover costs but also generate revenue.

Post-Show Sales: Capitalize on the excitement generated by your fashion show by offering attendees the opportunity to purchase the showcased items.

Collaborations and Partnerships

Collaborations and partnerships can significantly enhance your brand's distribution reach and credibility.

Influencer Collaborations: Partner with fashion influencers to promote your brand. Influencers can help you reach a broader and engaged audience.

Fashion Retailer Collaborations: Collaborate with established fashion retailers to create exclusive collections or co-branded products. This can introduce your brand to a larger customer base.

Cross-Industry Partnerships: Explore partnerships with complementary brands outside of the fashion industry. For instance, collaborations with beauty or lifestyle brands can open up new avenues for distribution.

Retailer Pop-Ups: Work with established retailers to organize pop-up shops featuring your products in their stores. This provides exposure and access to their customer base.

Charity and Event Collaborations: Partner with charitable organizations or participate in fashion events to boost your brand's visibility and reputation.

Online Marketplaces: Collaborate with e-commerce marketplaces to expand your online presence and reach a wider audience.

Collaborations and partnerships offer opportunities for cross-promotion and reaching new customer segments, allowing you to tap into established distribution channels and customer bases.

Building distribution channels for your fashion startup is essential for growth. By strategically implementing retail and wholesale strategies, organizing pop-up shops and fashion shows, and fostering collaborations and partnerships, you can diversify your distribution channels and extend your brand's reach. These efforts contribute to increased visibility, customer engagement, and sales, all of which are essential for the success and expansion of your fashion brand.

CHAPTER 11: INVENTORY MANAGEMENT AND SUPPLY CHAIN

Efficient inventory management and a well-structured supply chain are critical aspects of running a successful fashion startup. In this chapter, we'll explore effective inventory control, sustainable practices in the fashion industry, and strategies for streamlining your supply chain.

Effective Inventory Control

Inventory control is crucial in fashion because it directly impacts your business's cash flow, profitability, and customer satisfaction. Here are key principles for managing your inventory effectively:

Demand Forecasting: Use historical sales data and market trends to predict product demand accurately. This minimizes overstocking or understocking issues.

Stock Turnover: Measure how quickly you sell and replace your inventory. A high stock turnover ratio indicates efficient inventory management.

Just-in-Time (JIT) Inventory: Implement JIT inventory practices to minimize holding costs. With JIT, you order goods only as needed to meet customer demand.

ABC Analysis: Categorize your products into A, B, and C groups based on their importance and demand. Allocate resources and attention accordingly.

Safety Stock: Maintain a safety stock level to prepare for unexpected demand fluctuations or supply disruptions.

Inventory Tracking: Use inventory management software to track your stock levels, sales, and reordering needs in real time.

Returns and Excess Inventory: Develop a strategy for handling returns and dealing with excess inventory. Consider clearance sales, donations, or recycling options.

Supplier Communication: Maintain open communication with your suppliers to ensure timely deliveries and accurate order fulfillment.

Stock Rotation: Rotate older stock to the front to encourage the sale of older items first.

Audit and Reevaluate: Regularly audit your inventory and reevaluate your stocking decisions to adjust to market changes.

Effective inventory control helps you reduce carrying costs, minimize the risk of obsolete stock, and ensure that your customers find the products they want when they want them.

Sustainable Practices in Fashion

Sustainability is a growing concern in the fashion industry. Embracing eco-friendly and ethical practices not only benefits the environment but also appeals to a conscious consumer base. Here are some sustainable practices to consider:

Sustainable Materials: Choose sustainable and ethically sourced materials for your clothing. Organic cotton, recycled fabrics, and eco-friendly dyes are excellent options.

Reduce Waste: Minimize fabric waste during production by optimizing pattern layouts and recycling scraps.

Ethical Manufacturing: Partner with manufacturers and suppliers who follow ethical labor practices and have transparent supply chains.

Eco-Friendly Packaging: Use recyclable, biodegradable, or reusable packaging materials to minimize your brand's environmental footprint.

Reduced Water Usage: Adopt water-saving techniques in fabric dyeing and production processes to reduce water consumption.

Energy Efficiency: Use energy-efficient technologies and processes in your manufacturing and distribution.

Slow Fashion: Promote slow fashion by creating timeless, durable pieces that stand the test of time rather than following fast fashion trends.

Transparency: Be transparent about your supply chain and sustainable practices. Educate customers about your brand's commitment to eco-friendliness.

Recycling Programs: Offer recycling programs where customers can return old clothing for reuse or recycling.

Sustainable practices not only resonate with an environmentally conscious audience but also position your brand as a responsible and ethical player in the fashion industry.

Streamlining Your Supply Chain

A well-organized supply chain is the backbone of your fashion business. To streamline it, consider the following strategies:

Supplier Selection: Carefully select reliable suppliers who can meet your quality and timeliness standards.

Supplier Relationships: Build strong relationships with your suppliers based on trust and communication.

Centralized Inventory: Maintain centralized control over your inventory to minimize inefficiencies and reduce costs.

Technology Integration: Implement technology solutions like Enterprise Resource Planning (ERP) systems for better visibility and management of your supply chain.

Quality Control: Establish quality control measures to ensure that your products meet the highest standards.

Distribution Centers: Consider using distribution centers strategically located to minimize shipping costs and reduce delivery times.

Collaboration with 3PLs: Collaborate with third-party logistics providers (3PLs) for efficient order fulfillment and shipping.

Data Analytics: Use data analytics to identify inefficiencies and bottlenecks in your supply chain and make data-driven improvements.

Resilience Planning: Develop contingency plans for supply chain disruptions, such as natural disasters or political events.

By streamlining your supply chain, you can reduce costs, improve delivery times, and ensure the smooth operation of your fashion business.

Efficient inventory management, sustainable practices, and a streamlined supply chain are integral to your fashion startup's success. Implementing these strategies ensures that your products are readily available to customers, reduces the environmental impact of your operations, and optimizes your business processes. These practices contribute not only to your brand's growth but also to its reputation as a responsible and efficient player in the fashion industry.

CHAPTER 12: SALES AND CUSTOMER RELATIONS

Effective sales strategies and exceptional customer service are pivotal to the growth and success of your fashion startup. In this chapter, we will explore sales strategies tailored to fashion startups, the significance of providing excellent customer service, and the steps for building a loyal customer base.

Sales Strategies for Fashion Startups

Fashion startups require specialized sales strategies to differentiate themselves in a competitive market. Here are key strategies to consider:

Brand Storytelling: Use compelling brand narratives to connect with customers emotionally. Share the story behind your brand, your mission, and what makes your products unique.

Multi-Channel Sales: Sell your products through various channels, including your online store, pop-up shops, and collaborations with retail partners.

Limited Editions and Exclusivity: Create limited-edition collections or exclusive designs to generate excitement and urgency among customers.

Pricing and Promotions: Set competitive pricing, but don't shy away from premium pricing if your brand supports it. Offer promotions and discounts strategically.

Customer Engagement: Engage with customers on social media, through email marketing, and at events. Respond promptly to inquiries and build relationships.

Product Demonstrations: Showcase your products through fashion shows, video content, and influencer partnerships to demonstrate their appeal and quality.

Personalization: Tailor your marketing and product recommendations based on customer preferences and browsing history.

Cross-Selling and Upselling: Encourage customers to purchase complementary items or upgrade their selections for a more complete ensemble.

Loyalty Programs: Implement customer loyalty programs that reward repeat customers with discounts, exclusive access, or early releases.

Customer Feedback: Act on customer feedback and use it to improve your products and customer experience continually.

Customer Service Excellence

Exceptional customer service sets fashion startups apart. Here are the principles of providing excellent customer service:

Responsive Communication: Respond to customer inquiries promptly and professionally, whether through email, chat, or phone.

Knowledgeable Staff: Ensure your staff is well-informed about your products, policies, and brand identity.

Efficient Returns and Exchanges: Make your return and exchange process straightforward and hassle-free for customers.

Personalization: Personalize interactions with customers, remembering their preferences and order history.

Conflict Resolution: Develop effective conflict resolution strategies to address customer concerns and issues swiftly.

Consistency: Ensure that all customers receive a consistent level of service, regardless of the channel they use to contact you.

Transparency: Be transparent about policies, shipping times, and any potential delays. Customers appreciate honesty.

Feedback Channels: Encourage customers to provide feedback and use their insights to improve your service.

Post-Purchase Engagement: Follow up with customers after their purchases to gather feedback and offer assistance if needed.

Empower Your Team: Empower your customer service team to make decisions and resolve issues without escalating them unnecessarily.

Providing excellent customer service not only retains customers but can also lead to positive word-of-mouth marketing, which is invaluable for a fashion startup.

Building a Loyal Customer Base

A loyal customer base is the foundation of a successful fashion business. Here's how to build and nurture a loyal customer following:

Consistent Branding: Maintain a consistent brand identity, messaging, and visual elements to create a recognizable brand.
Exceptional Quality: Ensure that your products meet or exceed customer expectations in terms of quality and design.

Engagement and Interaction: Regularly engage with your customers on social media, respond to comments, and initiate conversations.

Email Marketing: Implement email marketing campaigns to keep customers informed about new products, promotions, and exclusive events.

Exclusive Access: Provide loyal customers with early access to new collections, exclusive discounts, and limited-edition items.

Loyalty Programs: Create a loyalty program that rewards customers for repeat purchases and referrals.

Personal Thank-Yous: Show appreciation by sending personal thank-you notes or tokens of gratitude with orders.

Customer Feedback Loop: Continually gather customer feedback and use it to enhance your products and services.

Consistent Communication: Keep customers in the loop regarding your brand's activities, such as collaborations, events, and charitable contributions.

Community Building: Foster a sense of community among your customers. Encourage them to share their experiences and connect with each other.

Building a loyal customer base takes time and effort, but the results are worth it. Loyal customers not only return for repeat purchases but become brand advocates, spreading positive word-of-mouth and contributing to your brand's long-term success.

CHAPTER 13: FINANCIAL MANAGEMENT

Sound financial management is vital for the stability and growth of your fashion startup. In this chapter, we'll delve into managing cash flow effectively, understanding and using financial metrics and key performance indicators (KPIs), and the importance of budgeting and financial planning.

Managing Cash Flow

Cash flow management is the lifeblood of your fashion startup. It ensures that you have the resources to cover your expenses and investments. Here's how to manage your cash flow effectively:

Detailed Cash Flow Statement: Create a detailed cash flow statement that tracks the movement of money in and out of your business. This includes income, expenses, and investments.

Revenue Projections: Project your revenue realistically and ensure it aligns with your sales forecasts.

Expense Management: Carefully manage your expenses by prioritizing essential costs and trimming unnecessary spending.

Payment Terms: Negotiate favorable payment terms with suppliers and vendors to match your cash flow patterns.

Inventory Control: Optimize your inventory to prevent overstocking and reduce holding costs.

Contingency Planning: Develop contingency plans for unexpected expenses or revenue shortfalls.

Working Capital: Maintain adequate working capital to cover day-to-day operational costs.

Invoice Promptly: Invoice customers promptly and encourage timely payments.

Credit Management: Monitor credit extended to customers to minimize bad debt.

Cash Reserves: Build up cash reserves to provide a safety net in case of unforeseen circumstances.

Effective cash flow management ensures that your business remains solvent, can take advantage of growth opportunities, and is well-prepared for unexpected financial challenges.

Financial Metrics and KPIs

Financial metrics and key performance indicators (KPIs) provide insights into the financial health and performance of your fashion startup. Here are some critical metrics to track:

Gross Profit Margin: Calculate the gross profit margin to understand the profitability of your products.

Net Profit Margin: Measure the net profit margin to assess the overall profitability of your business.

Return on Investment (ROI): Evaluate the ROI for marketing campaigns, product launches, and other investments.

Inventory Turnover: Determine how quickly your inventory is sold and replaced.

Customer Acquisition Cost: Calculate the cost of acquiring a new customer, which should be lower than the customer's lifetime value.

Accounts Receivable Days: Track the average number of days it takes to collect payments from customers.

Accounts Payable Days: Monitor the average number of days it takes to pay your suppliers.

Debt-to-Equity Ratio: Assess your business's financial leverage and ability to cover debt obligations.

Current Ratio: Determine your business's ability to meet its short-term liabilities.

Return on Assets (ROA): Measure the efficiency of your asset utilization in generating profit.

Understanding and regularly analyzing these financial metrics and KPIs empowers you to make data-driven decisions, identify areas for improvement, and monitor the financial health of your business.

Budgeting and Financial Planning

Budgeting and financial planning are critical components of financial management. They help you set clear financial goals and allocate resources effectively. Here's how to approach budgeting and financial planning:

Annual Budget: Create an annual budget that outlines expected revenues and expenses for the upcoming year.

Break-Even Analysis: Determine your break-even point to understand when your business becomes profitable.

Forecasting: Develop financial forecasts that project your income, expenses, and cash flow for the short-term and long-term.

Expense Control: Analyze historical data and trends to control and optimize your expenses.

Scenario Planning: Develop scenarios for best-case and worst-case financial situations to prepare for uncertainties.

Investment Planning: Plan investments strategically, including marketing, product development, and expansion.

Emergency Fund: Maintain an emergency fund to cover unexpected expenses.

Regular Review: Review and update your budget and financial plan regularly to adapt to changing circumstances.

Financial planning allows you to make informed decisions about the allocation of resources, set realistic financial goals, and ensure that your business remains on a sustainable and growth-oriented path.

Effectively managing cash flow, understanding financial metrics and KPIs, and implementing budgeting and financial planning are essential for the success and sustainability of your fashion startup. By prioritizing these aspects of financial management, you can make well-informed decisions, respond to financial challenges proactively, and position your business for long-term growth and profitability.

CHAPTER 14: SCALING YOUR FASHION BUSINESS

Scaling your fashion business is an exciting but challenging endeavor. In this chapter, we'll explore strategies for expanding your product lines, entering new markets, and the associated growth strategies and challenges.

Expanding Product Lines

Expanding your product lines is a common way to scale a fashion business. Here are key considerations:

Diversification: Consider offering a broader range of products within your niche. For example, if you focus on casual wear, you might expand into formal wear or accessories.

Market Research: Conduct thorough market research to identify gaps and opportunities in your product offerings. What do your existing customers want, and what can you introduce to attract new ones?

Design Consistency: Maintain a consistent design aesthetic across new product lines to align with your brand identity.

Quality Assurance: Ensure the same level of quality in new products as in your existing lines.

Limited Editions: Use limited-edition releases to generate buzz and excitement around new product launches.

Cross-Promotion: Promote new product lines to your existing customer base through email marketing, social media, and your website.

Testing the Waters: Start with a limited selection to test the market's response before scaling up production.

Entering New Markets

Expanding into new markets, whether geographically or demographically, is a significant growth opportunity. Here's how to approach it:

Market Analysis: Thoroughly research the new market to understand its demographics, preferences, and competitive landscape.

Local Partnerships: Collaborate with local retailers, influencers, or fashion events to establish a presence in the new market.

Cultural Sensitivity: Be culturally sensitive when marketing to a new audience. Your brand message and design choices should resonate with local customs and trends.

Local Regulations: Familiarize yourself with local regulations and customs procedures if expanding internationally.

Localization: Consider offering products tailored to the new market's specific needs and preferences.

Language and Customer Support: Provide customer support in the local language and offer localized customer experiences.

Market Entry Strategy: Decide whether to enter the market through e-commerce, local retail partnerships, or by opening your own stores.

Growth Strategies and Challenges

Scaling your fashion business requires thoughtful strategies and an awareness of potential challenges. Here are some growth strategies and how to tackle challenges:

E-commerce Expansion: Expand your online presence and consider launching e-commerce platforms in different markets.

Flagship Stores: Open flagship stores in high-traffic areas or fashion capitals to build brand recognition.

Sustainable Growth: Focus on sustainable growth to avoid overextending your resources.

Investment and Financing: Secure the necessary capital through investment or loans to fund your expansion plans.

Operational Efficiency: Optimize your operations to handle increased demand and maintain efficiency.

Brand Consistency: Ensure that your brand's core message and identity remain consistent as you scale.

Market Adaptation: Be prepared to adapt to local market conditions and customer expectations.

Competition: Keep a close eye on the competitive landscape and adjust your strategies accordingly.

Supply Chain Optimization: Continually optimize your supply chain to meet the demands of growth.

Talent Acquisition: Attract and retain talented professionals who can help drive your business forward.

Scaling your fashion business is a dynamic and complex process, but with the right strategies and a clear understanding of the potential challenges, you can achieve sustainable growth and expand your brand's reach. By diversifying your product lines, entering new markets, and implementing growth strategies, you can position your fashion business for long-term success.

Chapter 15: Sustainability and Ethical Fashion

The fashion industry is increasingly recognizing the importance of sustainability and ethical practices. In this chapter, we will explore the significance of embracing sustainable practices, the importance of ethical sourcing and production, and the future of sustainable fashion.

Embracing Sustainable Practices

Sustainability in fashion involves reducing the industry's environmental impact and embracing ethical practices. Here's how to do it:

Eco-Friendly Materials: Choose sustainable and eco-friendly materials, such as organic cotton, hemp, Tencel, and recycled fabrics.

Reducing Waste: Minimize waste during production by optimizing pattern layouts and recycling fabric scraps.

Ethical Manufacturing: Partner with manufacturers and suppliers who follow ethical labor practices, maintain transparent supply chains, and prioritize worker well-being.

Eco-Friendly Dyes: Use eco-friendly and low-impact dyes to minimize chemical pollution and water usage.

Sustainable Packaging: Utilize eco-friendly packaging materials, such as recyclable, biodegradable, or reusable options.

Reduced Carbon Footprint: Implement energy-efficient technologies in manufacturing and distribution to reduce your brand's carbon footprint.

Transparency: Be transparent about your supply chain and the sustainable practices you employ. Educate your customers about your commitment to eco-friendliness.

Sustainable Collections: Create sustainable fashion collections, featuring products designed for durability, quality, and timeless appeal.

Ethical Sourcing and Production

Ethical fashion involves the fair treatment of all individuals involved in the production process. Here's how to ensure ethical sourcing and production:

Fair Wages: Ensure that workers, including those in your supply chain, receive fair wages that meet or exceed local minimum wage standards.

Safe Working Conditions: Guarantee safe and healthy working conditions for all employees, whether in your own manufacturing facilities or those of your suppliers.

No Child Labor: Strictly prohibit child labor in your supply chain, complying with international labor standards.

Supply Chain Transparency: Maintain a transparent supply chain, working only with manufacturers and suppliers who share your commitment to ethical practices.

Social Responsibility: Engage in social responsibility programs, such as supporting worker welfare initiatives, education, or health services for employees.

Worker Empowerment: Empower workers to voice their concerns and provide a safe platform for addressing issues.

Regular Audits: Regularly audit your supply chain to ensure that ethical practices are upheld.

The Future of Sustainable Fashion

Sustainable fashion is the future of the industry. Here's what you can expect in the realm of sustainable fashion:

Innovative Materials: Continued development of innovative and sustainable materials, such as lab-grown leather and biodegradable textiles.

Circular Fashion: A shift toward circular fashion, where products are designed for recycling, reuse, and extended lifecycles.

Secondhand and Vintage: A growing market for secondhand and vintage clothing, promoting sustainability through reuse.

Sustainable Technologies: Adoption of sustainable technologies like 3D knitting and zero-waste pattern cutting.

Regulations and Standards: The establishment of more stringent regulations and industry standards for sustainable and ethical practices.

Consumer Awareness: An increasingly aware and demanding consumer base that prioritizes ethical and sustainable brands.

Collaborations: Collaborations between fashion brands, influencers, and sustainable organizations to promote eco-friendly practices.

The future of fashion is green, and embracing sustainability and ethical practices isn't just a trend; it's a necessity. By incorporating sustainable materials, ethical sourcing, and promoting eco-conscious practices, your fashion brand can not only contribute to a more sustainable future but also align with the evolving values and expectations of today's consumers.